LOW PURINE

COOKBOOK AND FOOD LIST
FOR GOUT PATIENTS

Low purine recipes for gout sufferers to live
a happier and healthier Life

Dr. ELIZABETH PHILIP

Table of Contents

Chapter 1

Understanding Gout and the Role of a Low Purine Diet

What is Gout?

Gout is a painful and inflammatory form of arthritis caused by the buildup of uric acid crystals in joints, often affecting the big toe. Uric acid, a waste product from the breakdown of purines (found in some foods and produced by the body), should be excreted through the kidneys. However, in gout, there's either excessive uric acid production or inefficient elimination, leading to crystallization in joints.

Gout attacks are characterized by sudden and severe pain, redness, swelling, and warmth in the affected joint. These episodes can be triggered by factors like dietary choices (high-purine foods and alcohol), dehydration, obesity, and certain medical conditions.

Diagnosis typically involves assessing symptoms, measuring uric acid levels in the blood, and sometimes analyzing joint fluid. Treatment includes managing acute attacks with medications like NSAIDs, colchicine, or corticosteroids, followed by long-term strategies to lower uric acid levels. Lifestyle changes, such as dietary modifications and maintaining a healthy weight, are essential to prevent future attacks.

Untreated gout can lead to joint damage and complications like kidney stones. Proper management aims to reduce symptoms, minimize flare-ups, and improve the overall well-being of individuals with gout.

How Does it Affect the Body?

Gout, a painful and complex form of arthritis, has a profound impact on the body beyond joint pain. It stems from the accumulation of uric acid crystals in joints, leading to recurrent attacks of inflammation. The consequences extend throughout the body:

Gout's most apparent impact is on joints, causing intense pain, swelling, and redness, primarily affecting the big toe but also other joints. Repeated gout attacks can result in joint damage and deformities, impairing mobility.

Kidneys may be affected as well, with high uric acid levels leading to kidney stone formation, which can cause excruciating pain and potentially harm kidney function.

11

Gout is associated with systemic health issues. Chronic inflammation can contribute to heart disease, hypertension, and metabolic syndrome, increasing the risk of heart attacks and strokes.

Mentally, living with gout can be taxing. The unpredictability of attacks, constant pain, and potential disability can lead to emotional distress, anxiety, and depression.

Daily life is disrupted by gout. Physical activities become limited, sleep is disturbed due to nighttime attacks, and relationships and routines can suffer. Tophi, which are hard uric acid deposits beneath the skin, can develop if gout remains untreated, further affecting the body's appearance and comfort.

In essence, gout's impact extends far beyond joint pain, affecting physical health, emotional well-being, and overall quality of life. Proper management through medication, dietary changes, and lifestyle adjustments is vital to minimize these effects and improve the well-being of those living with gout.

How Does a Low Purine Diet Help Manage Gout?

When there is an excess of uric acid in the body, it can accumulate in the joints, leading to gout attacks. To reduce the occurrence and severity of gout attacks, one can lower uric acid levels by decreasing the consumption of foods rich in purines, such as red meat, organ meats, seafood, and specific vegetables like asparagus and mushrooms.

A low-purine diet typically incorporates lean protein sources like poultry, low-fat dairy products, and plant-based proteins such as beans and lentils. It also emphasizes the inclusion of whole grains, fruits, and vegetables that are low in purines.

It's important to note that while adopting a low-purine diet can assist in managing gout, it should be complemented by other lifestyle modifications like maintaining proper hydration, achieving and sustaining a healthy weight, and engaging in regular physical activity.

Chapter 2

The Science Behind a Low Purine Diet

What are Purines and How Do They Affect Gout?

Purines are nitrogen-containing compounds that occur naturally in the body and many foods. They are essential building blocks for DNA, RNA, and various cellular processes. The body also produces uric acid as a byproduct when purines are broken down.

While purines have important functions in the body, excessive intake of purine-rich foods can lead to high levels of uric acid in the bloodstream. When there is too much uric acid in the body, it can form crystals that deposit in the joints, leading to gout and other health problems.

In addition to certain foods, other factors can contribute to high levels of uric acid in the body, such as certain medical conditions, medications, and genetics.

In summary, purines are compounds that are important for various physiological processes in the body but can contribute to health problems when their intake is excessive. It's important to maintain a balanced diet and work with a healthcare professional to determine an appropriate intake of purine-containing foods based on individual health status and needs.

The Link Between Purines, Uric Acid, and Gout

Uric acid is a waste product that forms when the body breaks down purines. Purines are naturally occurring compounds that can be found in various foods, such as red meat, seafood, and certain vegetables.

Normally, uric acid is excreted from the body through the kidneys. However, if there are elevated levels of uric acid in the blood, urate crystals can form and accumulate in the joints. This can result in a painful condition known as gout.

As such, there is a connection between uric acid, purines, and gout. Consuming a diet rich in purine-containing foods can elevate uric acid levels in the bloodstream, which increases the likelihood of developing gout. Conversely, a low-purine diet can be beneficial in managing gout symptoms by reducing uric acid production.

It is important to note that while purines are necessary for normal bodily functions, an excessive intake of purine-rich foods can increase the risk of developing gout. Therefore, seeking the advice of a healthcare professional to develop an individualized treatment plan is essential in effectively managing gout.

How a Low Purine Diet Reduces Uric Acid Levels

A low-purine diet can help decrease the levels of uric acid in the body by limiting the consumption of purine-rich foods. These foods, once broken down during the metabolic process, result in uric acid production.

When uric acid levels become elevated, urate crystals can form in the joints, causing painful gout attacks. Reducing the intake of purine-rich foods can lower uric acid production, resulting in lower uric acid levels in the bloodstream.

A low-purine diet typically involves consuming foods that are low in purines, such as lean protein sources like poultry, low-fat dairy products, and plant-based proteins like beans and lentils. It also includes whole grains, fruits, and vegetables that are low in purines.

In addition to a low-purine diet, other lifestyle modifications can aid in managing gout symptoms and reducing uric acid levels in the body. These include staying well-hydrated, maintaining a healthy weight, and engaging in regular physical activity. Medications may also be required in some cases to manage gout symptoms and reduce uric acid levels.

To sum up, a low-purine diet is a useful strategy for reducing uric acid levels in the body, which can help manage gout symptoms. Seeking guidance from a healthcare professional to establish a personalized treatment plan is critical for effectively managing gout and promoting overall health.

Chapter 3

Low purine food list

A low-purine diet is often recommended for individuals with gout or those at risk of developing gout to help reduce the frequency of gout attacks. Purines are natural compounds found in some foods, and when they break down, they can produce uric acid, which may contribute to gout.

Food to eat on a Low-Purine Diet:

Low-Purine Proteins:

- Lean cuts of poultry (e.g., skinless chicken and turkey)
- Eggs (limit yolks)
- Plant-based proteins (e.g., tofu, tempeh, and legumes)

Dairy and Dairy Alternatives:

- Low-fat or fat-free milk and yogurt
- Plant-based milk alternatives (e.g., almond or soy milk)

Whole Grains:

- Oats
- Brown rice
- Quinoa
- Whole wheat pasta
- Barley

Fruits (Low-Purine):

- Cherries (known to reduce gout attacks)
- Apples
- Berries (e.g., strawberries, blueberries, and raspberries)
- Citrus fruits (e.g., oranges and grapefruits)

Vegetables (Low-Purine):

- Leafy greens (e.g., spinach and kale)
- Bell peppers
- Cabbage
- Cauliflower
- Potatoes

Nuts and Seeds (in moderation):

- Almonds
- Walnuts
- Chia seeds
- Flaxseeds

Beverages:

- Water (hydration is crucial for gout management)
- Herbal teas (e.g., chamomile or ginger tea)

Foods to Limit or Avoid on a low Purine Diet:

High-Purine Meats:

- Organ meats (liver, kidney, sweetbreads)
- Game meats (venison, elk, and bear)
- Processed meats (sausages, hot dogs, bacon)
- Gravy made from meat drippings

Seafood High in Purines:

- Anchovies
- Sardines
- Mussels
- Scallops
- Herring
- Trout
- Caviar

High-Purine Vegetables:

- Spinach

24

- Asparagus
- Cauliflower
- Mushrooms
- Peas
- Lentils
- Beans (dried beans, soybeans)

Beverages:

- Alcohol, especially beer and liquor
- High-fructose corn syrup-containing drinks (soda)
- Excessive coffee and tea (limit to moderate consumption)

High-Purine Grains and Cereals:

- Whole grain products like whole wheat bread and oatmeal (consumed in moderation)
- Bran cereals

Certain Fruits:

- Limit consumption of some fruits, such as:
- Strawberries
- Blueberries
- Raspberries

High-Purine Condiments and Sauces:

- Gravy (meat-based)
- Bouillon cubes or broths made from high-purine meats

Miscellaneous Items:

- Yeast extract spreads (Marmite, Vegemite)
- High-purine sauces like Worcestershire sauce

Limit Sweets and Desserts:

- High-fructose corn syrup-containing sweets

26

- Excessive consumption of cakes, pastries, and sugary desserts

Processed Foods:

- Some processed foods may contain hidden sources of purines, so it's essential to read labels carefully.

Fried and Fatty Foods:

- High-fat diets may increase purine production, so it's advisable to limit fried and fatty foods.

Beer and Yeast Extracts:

- Beer contains purines and can raise uric acid levels. Yeast extract spreads like Marmite and Vegemite should also be avoided

High-Fat Dairy:

- High-fat dairy products like full-fat milk, cheese, and butter should be consumed in moderation.

Chapter 5

Breakfast Recipes

Oatmeal with Bananas and Almonds

Ingredients:

1/2 cup rolled oats

1 banana, sliced

2 tablespoons chopped almonds

1 teaspoon honey

Instructions:

- Cook the rolled oats according to package instructions.
- Top with sliced bananas and chopped almonds.
- Drizzle honey on top.
- Serve and enjoy!

Nutritional facts:

Calories: 352

Protein: 10g

Fat: 12g

Carbohydrates: 55g

Fiber: 8g

Sugar: 16g

Quinoa Breakfast Bowl

Ingredients:

1 cup cooked quinoa

1/2 cup sliced strawberries

1/4 cup chopped walnuts

1 tablespoon honey

Instructions:

- Combine cooked quinoa, sliced strawberries, and chopped walnuts in a bowl.
- Drizzle honey on top.
- Serve and enjoy!

Nutritional facts:

Calories: 358

Protein: 9g

Fat: 17g

Carbohydrates: 46g

Fiber: 6g

Sugar: 13g

Scrambled Eggs with Vegetables

Ingredients:

2 eggs

1/4 cup diced bell peppers

1/4 cup diced onions

1/4 cup sliced mushrooms

1 tablespoon olive oil

Instructions:

- Heat olive oil in a pan over medium heat.
- Add diced bell peppers, onions, and sliced mushrooms to the pan and sauté for a few minutes until tender.

- Beat the eggs in a separate bowl and pour them into the pan with the vegetables.
- Cook and scramble the eggs until fully cooked.
- Serve and enjoy!

Nutritional facts:

Calories: 263

Protein: 13g

Fat: 20g

Carbohydrates: 7g

Fiber: 1g

Sugar: 3g

Cottage Cheese with Pineapple

Ingredients:

1/2 cup low-fat cottage cheese

1/2 cup pineapple chunks

Instructions:

- Combine the low-fat cottage cheese and pineapple chunks in a bowl.
- Serve and enjoy!

Nutritional facts:

Calories: 121

Protein: 14g

Fat: 1g

Carbohydrates: 16g

Fiber: 1g

Sugar: 14g

Avocado Toast with Hard-Boiled Eggs

Ingredients:

1 slice of whole wheat bread

1/4 avocado, mashed

1 hard-boiled egg, sliced

Salt and pepper to taste

Instructions:

- Toast the bread.
- Spread mashed avocado on the toast.
- Top with a sliced hard-boiled egg.
- Season with salt and pepper to taste.
- Serve and enjoy!

Nutritional facts:

Calories: 268

Protein: 13g

Fat: 16g

Carbohydrates: 18g

Fiber: 6g

Sugar: 2g

Spinach and Feta Omelet

Ingredients:

2 eggs

1 cup spinach leaves

1/4 cup crumbled feta cheese

Salt and pepper to taste

1 tablespoon olive oil

Instructions:

- Heat olive oil in a pan over medium heat.
- Add spinach leaves to the pan and sauté for a few minutes until wilted.
- Beat the eggs in a separate bowl and pour them into the pan with the spinach.
- Sprinkle crumbled feta cheese on top.
- Cook the omelet until fully cooked.
- Season with salt and pepper to taste.
- Serve and enjoy!

Nutritional facts:

Calories: 293

Protein: 20g

Fat: 22g

Carbohydrates: 3g

Fiber: 1g

Sugar: 1g

Berry Chia Pudding

Ingredients:

1/4 cup chia seeds

1 cup unsweetened almond milk

1/2 cup mixed berries

1 tablespoon honey

Instructions:

- Combine chia seeds and almond milk in a bowl.
- Let it sit for 5 minutes until the mixture thickens.
- Top with mixed berries.
- Drizzle honey on top.
- Serve and enjoy!

Nutritional facts:

Calories: 254

Protein: 8g

Fat: 14g

Carbohydrates: 29g

Fiber: 14g

Sugar: 12g

Oatmeal with Blueberries and Almonds

Ingredients:

1/2 cup of rolled oats

1 cup of water

1/2 cup of blueberries

1 tablespoon of chopped almonds

1 tablespoon of honey (optional)

Instructions:

- In a small pot, bring the water to a boil.
- Add the rolled oats to the pot, and stir well.

- Reduce the heat to low, and let the oats cook for 5-7 minutes, stirring occasionally.
- Once the oatmeal has reached your desired consistency, remove it from the heat and transfer it to a bowl.
- Top the oatmeal with the blueberries and chopped almonds.
- Drizzle honey on top if desired.
- Serve hot and enjoy.

Nutritional Facts:

Calories: 296

Protein: 8g

Carbohydrates: 51g

Fat: 8g

Fiber: 9g

Scrambled Tofu with Spinach and Tomatoes

Ingredients:

1 package of firm tofu

1/2 cup of chopped spinach

1/2 cup of diced tomatoes

1/4 cup of diced onions

1 clove of minced garlic

1 tablespoon of olive oil

Salt and pepper to taste

Instructions:

• Drain and crumble the tofu into a bowl.

• In a pan, heat the olive oil over medium heat.

• Add the onions and garlic, and sauté until the onions are translucent.

39

- Add the crumbled tofu to the pan, and stir well to combine with the onions and garlic.
- Add the chopped spinach and diced tomatoes to the pan, and stir well to combine.
- Season with salt and pepper to taste, and continue cooking until the tofu is heated through and the spinach has wilted.
- Serve hot and enjoy.

Nutritional Facts:

Calories: 195

Protein: 14g

Carbohydrates: 9g

Fat: 13g

Fiber: 3g

Cottage Cheese with Pineapple and Walnuts

Ingredients:

1/2 cup of low-fat cottage cheese

1/2 cup of diced pineapple

1 tablespoon of chopped walnuts

Instructions:

- In a bowl, combine the cottage cheese and diced pineapple.
- Top the mixture with the chopped walnuts.
- Serve cold and enjoy.

Nutritional Facts:

Calories: 175

Protein: 16g

Carbohydrates: 19g

Fat: 5g

Fiber: 2g

Greek Yogurt with Berries and Granola

Ingredients:

1/2 cup of plain Greek yogurt

1/2 cup of mixed berries

1/4 cup of granola

Instructions:

- In a bowl, combine the Greek yogurt and mixed berries.
- Top the mixture with the granola.
- Serve cold and enjoy.

Nutritional Facts:

Calories: 241

Protein: 18g

Carbohydrates: 32g

Fat: 5g

Fiber: 5g

Chapter 5

Appetizers and Snacks

Greek Yogurt Dip

Ingredients:

1 cup plain Greek yogurt

1 garlic clove, minced

1 tablespoon lemon juice

1 tablespoon chopped fresh dill

Salt and pepper to taste

Instructions:

- In a bowl, mix the Greek yogurt, minced garlic, lemon juice, chopped fresh dill, salt, and pepper.
- Serve with sliced vegetables, such as carrots, cucumbers, and bell peppers.

43

Nutritional facts (per serving):

Calories: 50

Protein: 6 g

Fat: 0 g

Carbohydrates: 6 g

Fiber: 0 g

Grilled Zucchini and Eggplant

Ingredients:

1 medium zucchini, sliced

1 medium eggplant, sliced

1 tablespoon olive oil

Salt and pepper to taste

Instructions:

- Preheat a grill or grill pan to medium-high heat.
- In a bowl, toss the sliced zucchini and eggplant with olive oil, salt, and pepper.
- Grill the vegetables for 3-4 minutes on each side, until tender and lightly charred.
- Serve warm or at room temperature.

Nutritional facts (per serving):

Calories: 65

Protein: 1 g

Fat: 4 g

Carbohydrates: 8 g

Fiber: 4 g

Cucumber and Tomato Salad

Ingredients:

2 medium cucumbers, sliced

2 medium tomatoes, chopped

1/4 red onion, sliced

2 tablespoons olive oil

1 tablespoon red wine vinegar

Salt and pepper to taste

Instructions:

- In a bowl, mix the sliced cucumbers, chopped tomatoes, and sliced red onion.
- In a separate bowl, whisk together the olive oil, red wine vinegar, salt, and pepper.
- Pour the dressing over the cucumber and tomato mixture and toss to combine.
- Serve chilled.

Nutritional facts (per serving):

Calories: 72

Protein: 1 g

Fat: 7 g

Carbohydrates: 3 g

Fiber: 1 g

Baked Sweet Potato Fries

Ingredients:

2 medium sweet potatoes, peeled and cut into fries

1 tablespoon olive oil

1 teaspoon paprika

1/2 teaspoon garlic powder

Salt and pepper to taste

Instructions:

- Preheat the oven to 400°F.

- In a bowl, toss the sweet potato fries with olive oil, paprika, garlic powder, salt, and pepper.
- Spread the fries in a single layer on a baking sheet lined with parchment paper.
- Bake for 20-25 minutes, until crispy and golden brown.
- Serve hot.

Nutritional facts (per serving):

Calories: 95

Protein: 2 g

Fat: 3 g

Carbohydrates: 18 g

Fiber: 3 g

Roasted Chickpeas

Ingredients:

1 can chickpeas, drained and rinsed

1 tablespoon olive oil

1 teaspoon cumin

1/2 teaspoon garlic powder

Salt and pepper to taste

Instructions:

- Preheat the oven to 400°F.
- In a bowl, toss the chickpeas with olive oil, cumin, garlic powder, salt, and pepper.
- Spread the chickpeas in a single layer on a baking sheet lined with parchment paper.
- Bake for 25-30 minutes, stirring occasionally, until crispy and golden brown.
- Serve hot or at room temperature.

Nutritional facts (per serving):

Calories: 105

Protein: 4 g

Fat: 4 g

Carbohydrates: 14 g

Fiber: 4 g

Guacamole with Jicama Sticks

Ingredients:

2 ripe avocados, mashed

1 garlic clove, minced

1/4 red onion, chopped

1/4 cup chopped cilantro

1 tablespoon lime juice

Salt and pepper to taste

Jicama sticks, for dipping

Instructions:

- In a bowl, mix the mashed avocados, minced garlic, chopped red onion, chopped cilantro, lime juice, salt, and pepper.
- Serve with jicama sticks for dipping.

Nutritional facts (per serving):

Calories: 150

Protein: 2 g

Fat: 13 g

Carbohydrates: 10 g

Fiber: 7 g

Tuna Salad Lettuce Wraps

Ingredients:

1 can tuna, drained and flaked

1/4 red onion, chopped

1/4 cup chopped celery

1 tablespoon mayonnaise

1 tablespoon lemon juice

Salt and pepper to taste

Lettuce leaves, for wrapping

Instructions:

- In a bowl, mix the flaked tuna, chopped red onion, chopped celery, mayonnaise, lemon juice, salt, and pepper.
- Spoon the tuna salad onto lettuce leaves and wrap.
- Serve chilled.

Nutritional facts (per serving):

Calories: 100

Protein: 12 g

Fat: 4 g

Carbohydrates: 5 g

Fiber: 2 g

Salsa with Baked Tortilla Chips

Ingredients:

3 medium tomatoes, chopped

1/4 red onion, chopped

1 jalapeno pepper, seeded and chopped

2 tablespoons chopped cilantro tablespoon lime juice

Salt and pepper to taste

6 corn tortillas, cut into wedges

Instructions:

Preheat the oven to 375°F.

- In a bowl, mix the chopped tomatoes, chopped red onion, seeded and chopped jalapeno pepper, chopped cilantro, lime juice, salt, and pepper.
- Spread the tortilla wedges in a single layer on a baking sheet lined with parchment paper.
- Bake for 8-10 minutes, until crispy.
- Serve the tortilla chips with the salsa.

Nutritional facts (per serving):

Calories: 95

Protein: 3 g

Fat: 2 g

Carbohydrates: 19 g

Fiber: 4 g

Deviled Eggs with Smoked Salmon

Ingredients:

6 hard-boiled eggs, peeled and halved

1/4 cup Greek yogurt

1 tablespoon Dijon mustard

1 tablespoon chopped chives

2 oz smoked salmon, chopped

Salt and pepper to taste

Instructions:

In a bowl, mix the Greek yogurt, Dijon mustard, chopped chives, chopped smoked salmon, salt, and pepper.

Spoon the mixture into the halved hard-boiled egg whites.

Chill for at least 30 minutes before serving.

Nutritional facts (per serving):

Calories: 100

Protein: 9 g

Fat: 6 g

Carbohydrates: 2 g

Fiber: 0 g

Baked Zucchini Fries

Ingredients:

2 medium zucchini, cut into thin fries

1/4 cup grated Parmesan cheese

1/4 cup whole wheat breadcrumbs

1 tablespoon olive oil

Salt and pepper to taste

Instructions:

Preheat the oven to 425°F.

- In a bowl, mix the grated Parmesan cheese, whole wheat breadcrumbs, olive oil, salt, and pepper.
- Dip the zucchini fries in the breadcrumb mixture, pressing to coat.
- Place the coated zucchini fries in a single layer on a baking sheet lined with parchment paper.
- Bake for 15-20 minutes, until crispy and golden brown.
- Serve with low-purine ketchup or your favorite dipping sauce.

Nutritional facts (per serving):

Calories: 85

Protein: 5 g

Fat: 4 g

Carbohydrates: 9 g

Fiber: 2 g

Grilled Vegetable Skewers

Ingredients:

1 medium zucchini, sliced into rounds

1 medium yellow squash, sliced into rounds

1 red bell pepper, seeded and cut into chunks

1 yellow bell pepper, seeded and cut into chunks

1 red onion, cut into chunks

1 tablespoon olive oil

1 tablespoon balsamic vinegar

1 teaspoon dried oregano

Salt and pepper to taste

Wooden skewers, soaked in water for 30 minutes

Instructions:

- Preheat the grill to medium-high heat.
- Thread the sliced zucchini, sliced yellow squash, red bell pepper chunks, yellow bell pepper chunks, and red onion chunks onto the soaked wooden skewers.
- In a bowl, mix the olive oil, balsamic vinegar, dried oregano, salt, and pepper.
- Brush the vegetable skewers with the olive oil mixture.
- Grill the vegetable skewers for 10-15 minutes, turning occasionally, until charred and tender.
- Serve hot.

Nutritional facts (per serving):

Calories: 85

Protein: 2 g

Fat: 4 g

Carbohydrates: 13 g

Fiber: 4 g

Chapter 6

Main Dishes

Grilled Salmon with Lemon and Herbs

Ingredients:

4 salmon fillets (6 ounces each)

2 tablespoons olive oil

2 tablespoons chopped fresh herbs (such as dill, parsley, or basil)

1 lemon, sliced

Salt and pepper to taste

Instructions:

- Preheat the grill to medium-high heat.
- Brush the salmon fillets with olive oil and sprinkle with chopped herbs, salt, and pepper.

- Place the salmon fillets on the grill, skin-side down, and place the lemon slices on top.
- Grill the salmon for 8-10 minutes, until cooked through and flaky.
- Serve hot with additional lemon slices on the side.

Nutritional facts (per serving):

Calories: 320

Protein: 34 g

Fat: 19 g

Carbohydrates: 2 g

Fiber: 1 g

Roasted Chicken with Vegetables

Ingredients:

4 bone-in, skin-on chicken thighs

1 large sweet potato, peeled and cut into chunks

2 cups broccoli florets

1 red onion, cut into chunks

2 tablespoons olive oil

1 teaspoon dried thyme

Salt and pepper to taste

Instructions:

- Preheat the oven to 425°F.

- In a large bowl, toss the chicken thighs, sweet potato chunks, broccoli florets, and red onion chunks with olive oil, dried thyme, salt, and pepper.

- Spread the mixture in a single layer on a baking sheet.

- Roast for 30-35 minutes, until the chicken is cooked through and the vegetables are tender.

- Serve hot.

Nutritional facts (per serving):

Calories: 430

Protein: 33 g

Fat: 24 g

Carbohydrates: 22 g

Fiber: 4 g

Baked Cod with Tomatoes and Olives

Ingredients:

4 cod fillets (6 ounces each)

2 cups cherry tomatoes, halved

1/2 cup pitted Kalamata olives, halved

1/4 cup chopped fresh parsley

2 tablespoons olive oil

2 garlic cloves, minced

Salt and pepper to taste

Instructions:

- Preheat the oven to 375°F.
- In a large bowl, combine the cherry tomatoes, Kalamata olives, parsley, olive oil, minced garlic, salt, and pepper.

- Place the cod fillets in a baking dish and spoon the tomato and olive mixture over the top.
- Bake for 20-25 minutes, until the cod is cooked through and flaky.
- Serve hot.

Nutritional facts (per serving):

Calories: 300

Protein: 34 g

Fat: 12 g

Carbohydrates: 10 g

Fiber: 2 g

Grilled Turkey Burgers with Avocado and Tomato

Ingredients:

1 pound ground turkey

1/4 cup finely chopped red onion

1/4 cup finely chopped fresh parsley

1 tablespoon Worcestershire sauce

1 teaspoon garlic powder

Salt and pepper to taste

4 whole wheat burger buns

1 avocado, sliced

1 large tomato, sliced

4 lettuce leaves

Instructions:

- Preheat the grill to medium-high heat.
- In a large bowl, combine the ground turkey, chopped red onion, chopped parsley, Worcestershire sauce, garlic powder, salt, and pepper.
- Form the turkey mixture into 4 patties.
- Grill the turkey burgers for 5-6 minutes per side, or until cooked through.
- Toast the burger buns on the grill for 1-2 minutes.

- Assemble the burgers with the turkey patties, sliced avocado, sliced tomato, and lettuce leaves.
- Serve hot.

Nutritional facts (per serving):

Calories: 400

Protein: 34 g

Fat: 20 g

Carbohydrates: 25 g

Fiber: 6 g

Slow Cooker Chicken and Vegetables

Ingredients:

4 boneless, skinless chicken breasts (4-6 ounces each)

2 cups baby carrots

2 cups baby red potatoes, halved

1 large onion, chopped

2 garlic cloves, minced

1/2 cup low-sodium chicken broth

1/2 teaspoon dried thyme

Salt and pepper to taste

Instructions:

- Place the chicken breasts in the bottom of a slow cooker.
- Add the baby carrots, halved red potatoes, chopped onion, and minced garlic to the slow cooker.
- Pour the chicken broth over the top.
- Sprinkle the dried thyme, salt, and pepper over the top.
- Cover and cook on low for 6-8 hours, or until the chicken and vegetables are tender.
- Serve hot.

Nutritional facts (per serving):

Calories: 280

Protein: 31 g

Fat: 3 g

Carbohydrates: 30 g

Fiber: 4 g

Tuna and White Bean Salad

Ingredients:

2 (5-ounce) cans of chunk light tuna, drained

1 (15-ounce) can of white beans, drained and rinsed

1/2 cup chopped red onion

1/2 cup chopped fresh parsley

2 tablespoons olive oil

2 tablespoons red wine vinegar

Salt and pepper to taste

Instructions:

- In a large bowl, combine the drained tuna, white beans, chopped red onion, and chopped parsley.
- Drizzle the olive oil and red wine vinegar over the top.
- Season with salt and pepper to taste.
- Toss to combine all ingredients.
- Serve chilled or at room temperature.

Nutritional facts (per serving):

Calories: 320

Protein: 29 g

Fat: 11 g

Carbohydrates: 24 g

Fiber: 7 g

Baked Lemon Herb Salmon

Ingredients:

4 (4-6 ounce) salmon fillets

1 lemon, thinly sliced

2 tablespoons olive oil

2 tablespoons chopped fresh parsley

1 tablespoon chopped fresh dill

Salt and pepper to taste

Instructions:

- Preheat the oven to 400°F.
- Line a baking sheet with foil and lightly grease it with cooking spray.
- Place the salmon fillets on the prepared baking sheet.
  - Drizzle the olive oil over the salmon fillets.
  - Sprinkle the chopped fresh parsley and chopped fresh dill over the top.
  - Season with salt and pepper to taste.
  - Place a few thin lemon slices over each salmon fillet.
  - Bake for 12-15 minutes, or until the salmon is cooked through and flakes easily with a fork.

- Serve hot.

Nutritional facts (per serving):

Calories: 320

Protein: 31 g

Fat: 19 g

Carbohydrates: 3 g

Fiber: 1 g

Grilled Chicken and Vegetable Kebabs

Ingredients:

4 boneless, skinless chicken breasts (4-6 ounces each), cut into cubes

2 bell peppers, cut into chunks

1 red onion, cut into chunks

2 zucchini, cut into rounds

2 tablespoons olive oil

1 tablespoon chopped fresh rosemary

Salt and pepper to taste

Instructions:

- Preheat the grill to medium-high heat.
- Thread the chicken cubes, bell pepper chunks, red onion chunks, and zucchini rounds onto skewers.
- In a small bowl, whisk together the olive oil and chopped fresh rosemary.
- Brush the olive oil and rosemary mixture over the kebabs.
- Season with salt and pepper to taste.
- Grill the kebabs for 10-12 minutes, or until the chicken is cooked through and the vegetables are tender.
- Serve hot.

Nutritional facts (per serving):
Calories: 310
Protein: 32 g
Fat: 12 g

Carbohydrates: 15 g

Fiber: 4 g

Slow Cooker Beef Stew

Ingredients:

2 pounds of beef stew meat, cut into cubes

4 cups chopped mixed vegetables (such as carrots, celery, and onions)

2 garlic cloves, minced

4 cups of low-sodium beef broth

1 tablespoon tomato paste

1 teaspoon dried thyme

Salt and pepper to taste

Instructions:

• In a large slow cooker, combine the beef stew meat, chopped mixed vegetables, minced garlic, low-sodium beef broth, tomato paste, and dried thyme.

- Season with salt and pepper to taste.
- Cover and cook on low for 8-10 hours, or until the beef is tender and the vegetables are cooked through.
- Serve hot.

Nutritional facts (per serving):

Calories: 340

Protein: 34 g

Fat: 11 g

Carbohydrates: 24 g

Fiber: 5 g

Spinach and Mushroom Quiche

Ingredients:

1 refrigerated pie crust

1 tablespoon olive oil

1 small onion, diced

2 cups sliced mushrooms

2 cups fresh spinach leaves

4 large eggs

1 cup of low-fat milk

1/2 cup shredded Swiss cheese

Salt and pepper to taste

Instructions:

- Preheat the oven to 375°F.
- Place the refrigerated pie crust into a 9-inch pie dish.
- In a large skillet, heat the olive oil over medium-high heat.
- Add the diced onion and sliced mushrooms to the skillet and sauté for 5-7 minutes, or until the vegetables are tender.
- Add the fresh spinach leaves to the skillet and cook for an additional 1-2 minutes, or until the spinach is wilted.

- Remove the skillet from the heat and let cool for a few minutes.
- In a large bowl, whisk together the eggs and low-fat milk.
- Stir in the shredded Swiss cheese.
- Add the sautéed vegetables to the egg mixture and stir to combine.
- Season with salt and pepper to taste.
- Pour the egg and vegetable mixture into the prepared pie crust.
- Bake for 35-40 minutes, or until the quiche is set and golden brown.
- Let cool for a few minutes before slicing and serving.

Nutritional facts (per serving):

Calories: 260

Protein: 12 g

Fat: 16 g

Carbohydrates: 18 g

Fiber: 1 g

Turkey and Vegetable Chili

Ingredients:

1 pound ground turkey

1 onion, diced

2 garlic cloves, minced

1 red bell pepper, diced

2 zucchini, diced

2 cans (14.5 ounces each) of low-sodium diced tomatoes

1 can (15 ounces) of low-sodium kidney beans, drained and rinsed

1 tablespoon chili powder

1 teaspoon ground cumin

Salt and pepper to taste

Instructions:

- In a large pot or Dutch oven, cook the ground turkey over medium-high heat until browned and cooked through.
- Add the diced onion, minced garlic, diced red bell pepper, and diced zucchini to the pot and cook for 5-7 minutes, or until the vegetables are tender.
- Add the low-sodium diced tomatoes, drained and rinsed kidney beans, chili powder, and ground cumin to the pot.
- Season with salt and pepper to taste.
- Bring the chili to a simmer and cook for 20-30 minutes, or until the flavors have melded together and the vegetables are cooked through.
- Serve hot.

Nutritional facts (per serving):

Calories: 280

Protein: 25 g

Fat: 9 g

Carbohydrates: 25 g

Fiber: 8 g

Chapter 7

Side Dishes and Salads

Quinoa and Black Bean Salad

Ingredients:

1 cup quinoa

2 cups low-sodium vegetable broth

1 can (15 ounces) of low-sodium black beans, drained and rinsed

1 red bell pepper, diced

1/2 red onion, diced

1/4 cup chopped fresh cilantro

Juice of 1 lime

2 tablespoons olive oil

Salt and pepper to taste

Instructions:

- In a medium saucepan, bring the quinoa and vegetable broth to a boil.

- Reduce the heat to low, cover the saucepan, and simmer for 15-20 minutes, or until the quinoa is tender and the liquid is absorbed.
- In a large bowl, combine the cooked quinoa, drained and rinsed black beans, diced red bell pepper, diced red onion, and chopped fresh cilantro.
- In a small bowl, whisk together the lime juice, olive oil, salt, and pepper.
- Drizzle the lime dressing over the quinoa and black bean mixture and stir to combine.
- Serve at room temperature or chilled.

Nutritional facts (per serving):

Calories: 230

Protein: 8 g

Fat: 7 g

Carbohydrates: 34 g

Fiber: 9 g

Roasted Sweet Potato Wedges

Ingredients:

2 large sweet potatoes, peeled and cut into wedges

2 tablespoons olive oil

1 teaspoon paprika

1/2 teaspoon garlic powder

1/4 teaspoon cayenne pepper

Salt and pepper to taste

Instructions:

- Preheat the oven to 400°F.

- In a small bowl, whisk together the olive oil, paprika, garlic powder, cayenne pepper, salt, and pepper.

- Place the sweet potato wedges on a baking sheet.

- Drizzle the olive oil mixture over the sweet potato wedges and toss to coat.

- Roast for 20-25 minutes, or until the sweet potatoes are tender and lightly browned.
- Serve hot.

Nutritional facts (per serving):

Calories: 120

Protein: 2 g

Fat: 6 g

Carbohydrates: 17 g

Fiber: 3 g

Grilled Eggplant

Ingredients:

2 medium eggplants, cut into 1/2-inch slices

2 tablespoons olive oil

1 teaspoon dried oregano

1/2 teaspoon garlic powder

Salt and pepper to taste

Instructions:

- Preheat the grill to medium-high heat.
- In a small bowl, whisk together the olive oil, dried oregano, garlic powder, salt, and pepper.
- Brush the eggplant slices with the olive oil mixture on both sides.
- Grill the eggplant slices for 4-5 minutes per side or until tender and lightly charred.
- Serve hot.

Nutritional facts (per serving):

Calories: 70

Protein: 2 g

Fat: 4 g

Carbohydrates: 8 g

Fiber: 4 g

Tomato and Basil Salad

Ingredients:

2 large tomatoes, diced

1/4 cup chopped fresh basil

2 tablespoons balsamic vinegar

1 tablespoon olive oil

Salt and pepper to taste

Instructions:

- In a large bowl, combine the diced tomatoes and chopped fresh basil.
- In a small bowl, whisk together the balsamic vinegar, olive oil, salt, and pepper.
- Drizzle the balsamic dressing over the tomato mixture and toss to coat.
- Serve at room temperature.

Nutritional facts (per serving):

Calories: 50

Protein: 1 g

Fat: 3 g

Carbohydrates: 5 g

Fiber: 1 g

Roasted Asparagus

Ingredients:

1 pound fresh asparagus, tough ends trimmed
1 tablespoon olive oil
Salt and pepper to taste

Instructions:
- Preheat the oven to 400°F.
- Arrange the asparagus on a baking sheet.
- Drizzle with olive oil and season with salt and pepper to taste.
- Roast for 10-12 minutes, or until tender and lightly browned.
- Serve hot.

Nutritional facts (per serving):

Calories: 50

Protein: 3 g

Fat: 4 g

Carbohydrates: 4 g

Fiber: 2 g

Steamed Broccoli with Lemon and Parmesan

Ingredients:

1 pound fresh broccoli, trimmed and cut into florets

1 tablespoon olive oil

Juice of 1 lemon

1/4 cup grated Parmesan cheese

Salt and pepper to taste

Instructions:

- Fill a large pot with 1 inch of water and bring to a boil.

- Place the broccoli florets in a steamer basket and place the basket in the pot.
- Cover the pot and steam the broccoli for 5-7 minutes or until tender.
- In a large bowl, toss the steamed broccoli with the olive oil, lemon juice, grated Parmesan cheese, salt, and pepper.
- Serve hot.

Nutritional facts (per serving):

Calories: 80

Protein: 6 g

Fat: 4 g

Carbohydrates: 9 g

Fiber: 4 g

Grilled Asparagus

Ingredients:

1 pound fresh asparagus, trimmed

1 tablespoon olive oil

Salt and pepper to taste

Instructions:

- Preheat the grill to medium-high heat.
- Toss the trimmed asparagus with the olive oil, salt, and pepper.
- Grill the asparagus for 4-5 minutes per side or until tender and lightly charred.
- Serve hot

Nutritional facts (per serving):

Calories: 60

Protein: 3 g

Fat: 4 g

Carbohydrates: 5 g

Fiber: 3 g

Balsamic Roasted Carrots

Ingredients:

1 pound fresh carrots, peeled and sliced into 1/2-inch rounds

2 tablespoons olive oil

2 tablespoons balsamic vinegar

1 tablespoon honey

1 teaspoon dried thyme

Salt and pepper to taste

Instructions:

• Preheat the oven to 400°F.

• In a large bowl, whisk together the olive oil, balsamic vinegar, honey, dried thyme, salt, and pepper.

• Add the sliced carrots to the bowl and toss to coat.

• Spread the carrots out in a single layer on a baking sheet.

- Roast for 25-30 minutes, or until the carrots are tender and lightly browned.
- Serve hot.

Nutritional facts (per serving):

Calories: 90

Protein: 1 g

Fat: 5 g

Carbohydrates: 12 g

Fiber: 3 g

Caprese Salad

Ingredients:

1 large tomato, sliced

4 ounces fresh mozzarella cheese, sliced

2 tablespoons chopped fresh basil

1 tablespoon balsamic vinegar

1 tablespoon olive oil

Salt and pepper to taste

Instructions:

- Arrange the sliced tomato and mozzarella on a plate.
- Sprinkle the chopped fresh basil over the top.
- Drizzle the balsamic vinegar and olive oil over the salad.
- Season with salt and pepper to taste.
- Serve at room temperature.

Nutritional facts (per serving):

Calories: 210

Protein: 12 g

Fat: 16 g

Carbohydrates: 7 g

Fiber: 2 g

Roasted Brussels Sprouts

Ingredients:

1 pound Brussels sprouts, trimmed and halved

2 tablespoons olive oil

1 teaspoon garlic powder

Salt and pepper to taste

Instructions:

- Preheat the oven to 400°F.

- In a large bowl, toss together the Brussels sprouts, olive oil, garlic powder, salt, and pepper.

- Spread the Brussels sprouts out in a single layer on a baking sheet.

- Roast for 20-25 minutes, or until tender and lightly browned.

- Serve hot.

Nutritional facts (per serving):

Calories: 100

Protein: 4 g

Fat: 7 g

Carbohydrates: 9 g

Fiber: 4 g

Greek Salad

Ingredients:

2 cups chopped romaine lettuce

1/2 cup sliced cucumber

1/2 cup cherry tomatoes, halved

1/4 cup sliced red onion

1/4 cup crumbled feta cheese

2 tablespoons chopped kalamata olives

2 tablespoons olive oil

1 tablespoon red wine vinegar

1 teaspoon dried oregano

Salt and pepper to taste

Instructions:

• In a large bowl, combine the chopped romaine lettuce, sliced cucumber, cherry tomatoes, sliced red onion, crumbled feta cheese, and chopped kalamata olives.

- In a small bowl, whisk together the olive oil, red wine vinegar, dried oregano, salt, and pepper.
- Drizzle the dressing over the salad and toss to combine.
- Serve at room temperature.

Nutritional facts (per serving):

Calories: 170

Protein: 5 g

Fat: 14 g

Carbohydrates: 7 g

Fiber: 2 g

Chapter 9

Drinks

Pineapple-Basil Smoothie

Ingredients:

1 cup frozen pineapple

1/2 cup fresh basil leaves

1/2 cup unsweetened coconut milk

1/2 cup water

1/4 teaspoon vanilla extract

Instructions:

- Blend all ingredients in a blender until smooth.
- Serve and enjoy!

Nutritional Facts (per serving):

Calories: 102

Total Fat: 5g

Total Carbohydrates: 16g

Protein: 1g

Green Tea and Lemonade

Ingredients:

1 cup brewed green tea, chilled

1/2 cup fresh lemon juice

1/4 cup honey

2 cups water

Lemon slices for garnish

Instructions:

- Mix all ingredients in a pitcher.
- Serve chilled and garnish with lemon slices.

Nutritional Facts (per serving):

Calories: 63

Total Fat: 0g

Total Carbohydrates: 18g

Protein: 0g

Cucumber-Lemon Water

Ingredients:

1 medium cucumber, sliced

1 lemon, sliced

8 cups water

Ice cubes

Instructions:

- Combine cucumber and lemon slices in a pitcher.
- Add water and ice cubes.
- Let the mixture sit in the fridge for at least 1 hour before serving.

Nutritional Facts (per serving):

Calories: 2

Total Fat: 0g

Total Carbohydrates: 1g

Protein: 0g

Strawberry-Mint Infused Water

Ingredients:

1 cup sliced strawberries

1/4 cup fresh mint leaves

8 cups water

Ice cubes

Instructions:

- Combine strawberries and mint leaves in a pitcher.
- Add water and ice cubes.
- Let the mixture sit in the fridge for at least 1 hour before serving.

Nutritional Facts (per serving):

Calories: 2

Total Fat: 0g

Total Carbohydrates: 1g

Protein: 0g

Carrot-Orange Juice

Ingredients:

3 medium carrots, peeled and chopped

2 oranges, peeled and segmented

1/2 inch piece of ginger, peeled

1/2 cup water

Instructions:

- Combine all ingredients in a blender.
- Blend until smooth.
- Serve chilled.

Nutritional Facts (per serving):

Calories: 100

Total Fat: 0g

Total Carbohydrates: 25g

Protein: 2g

Blueberry-Lemon Smoothie

Ingredients:

1 cup frozen blueberries

1/2 cup fresh lemon juice

1/2 cup unsweetened almond milk

1/4 cup plain Greek yogurt

1 tablespoon honey

Instructions:

- Blend all ingredients in a blender until smooth.
- Serve and enjoy!

Nutritional Facts (per serving):

Calories: 147

Total Fat: 3g

Total Carbohydrates: 27g

Protein: 6g

Peach-Ginger Iced Tea

Ingredients:

2 cups brewed black tea, chilled

1 ripe peach, peeled and diced

1/2 inch piece of ginger, peeled

1/4 cup honey

1 cup ice cubes

Instructions:

- Combine all ingredients in a blender.
- Blend until smooth.
- Serve chilled.

Nutritional Facts (per serving):

Calories: 83

Total Fat: 0g

Total Carbohydrates: 22g

Protein: 1g

Mango-Coconut Water

Ingredients:

1 cup chopped mango

1 cup coconut water

1/2 cup water

1 tablespoon honey

1/4 teaspoon ground cardamom

Instructions:

- Combine all ingredients in a blender.
- Blend until smooth.
- Serve chilled.

Nutritional Facts (per serving):

Calories: 110

Total Fat: 1g

Total Carbohydrates: 27g

Protein: 2g

Berry-Limeade

Ingredients:

1/2 cup fresh lime juice

1/4 cup honey

1 cup mixed berries (strawberries, blueberries, raspberries)

3 cups water

Ice cubes

Instructions:

- Mix all ingredients in a pitcher.
- Serve chilled and garnish with additional berries if desired.

Nutritional Facts (per serving):

Calories: 58

Total Fat: 0g

Total Carbohydrates: 15g

Protein: 1g

Beet-Apple Juice

Ingredients:

2 medium beets, peeled and chopped

2 medium apples, peeled and chopped

1/2 inch piece of ginger, peeled

1/2 cup water

Instructions:

- Combine all ingredients in a blender.
- Blend until smooth.
- Serve chilled.

Nutritional Facts (per serving):

Calories: 129

Total Fat: 0g

Total Carbohydrates: 32g

Protein: 2g

Orange-Carrot-Ginger Juice

Ingredients:

3 medium carrots, peeled and chopped

2 oranges, peeled and segmented

1/2 inch piece of ginger, peeled

1/2 cup water

Instructions:

- Combine all ingredients in a blender.
- Blend until smooth.
- Serve chilled.

Nutritional Facts (per serving):

Calories: 100

Total Fat: 0g

Total Carbohydrates: 25g

Protein: 2g

Chapter 10:

Conclusion

Low Purine Cookbook and Food List for Gout Patients represents not just a culinary guide, but a transformative tool in the journey toward better health and improved quality of life for individuals living with gout. Throughout this comprehensive resource, we have explored the multifaceted aspects of gout management, focusing on the crucial role that diet plays in alleviating symptoms and preventing future flare-ups.

This cookbook and food list have empowered gout patients to take control of their condition by making informed dietary choices. By embracing the principles of a low-purine diet and incorporating the delicious and creative recipes provided, individuals can find enjoyment in their meals without compromising their health. We've seen how this cookbook has not only reduced the pain and discomfort associated with gout but also fostered a sense of well-being, confidence, and empowerment.

Moreover, the financial benefits of following a low-purine diet are undeniable. Gout-related medical expenses, including medications, doctor visits, and hospitalizations, can be significantly reduced when patients proactively manage their condition through dietary changes. The "Low Purine Cookbook and Food List for Gout Patients" has thus proven to be a wise investment in long-term healthcare savings, providing both immediate and long-lasting benefits to its users.

Furthermore, this cookbook has not only improved the physical health of gout patients but has also contributed to their overall mental and emotional well-being. By enjoying a variety of flavorful and satisfying low-purine meals, individuals have found renewed joy in eating and have experienced a positive impact on their mental outlook. This, in turn, has bolstered their resilience in managing gout and other health challenges.

In summary, the "Low Purine Cookbook and Food List for Gout Patients" is more than just a collection of recipes; it's a comprehensive resource that empowers individuals to regain control of their lives, enhance their health, and reduce their healthcare costs. By promoting a low-purine lifestyle that is both delicious and health-conscious, this cookbook has unlocked a path to a brighter, more vibrant future for those living with gout. As we reflect on the profitable impact it has made in terms of health, finances, and overall well-being, it is clear that this resource is not just a cookbook—it's a recipe for a better life.

Made in United States
North Haven, CT
25 February 2024

49204335R00065